We Can Do It!

**Written by
Marie Layson-Dale**

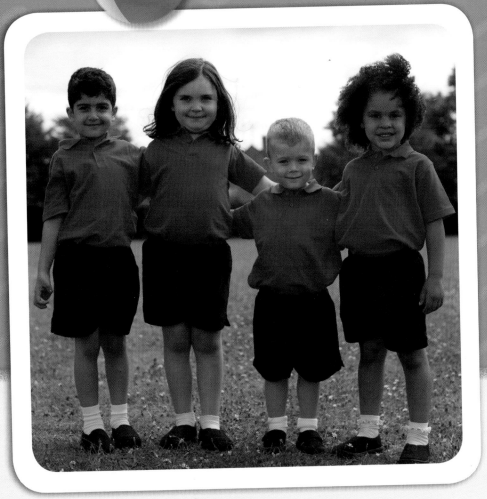

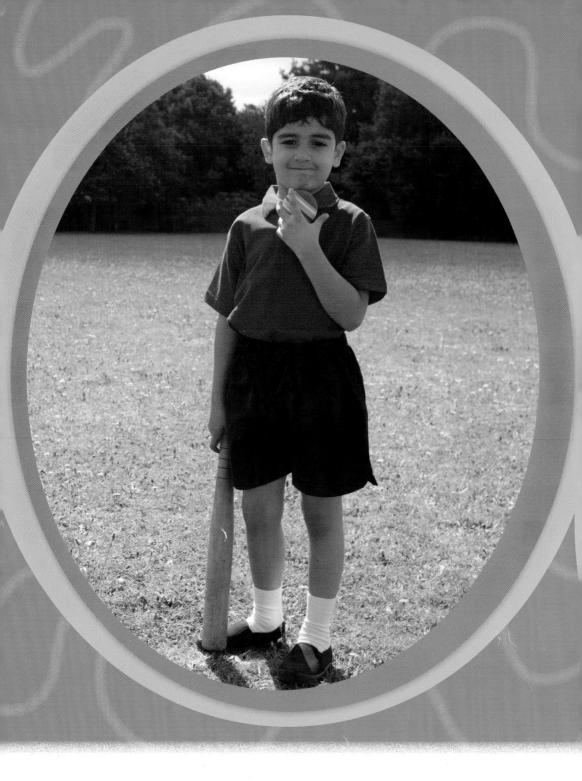

I can not hit this ball.

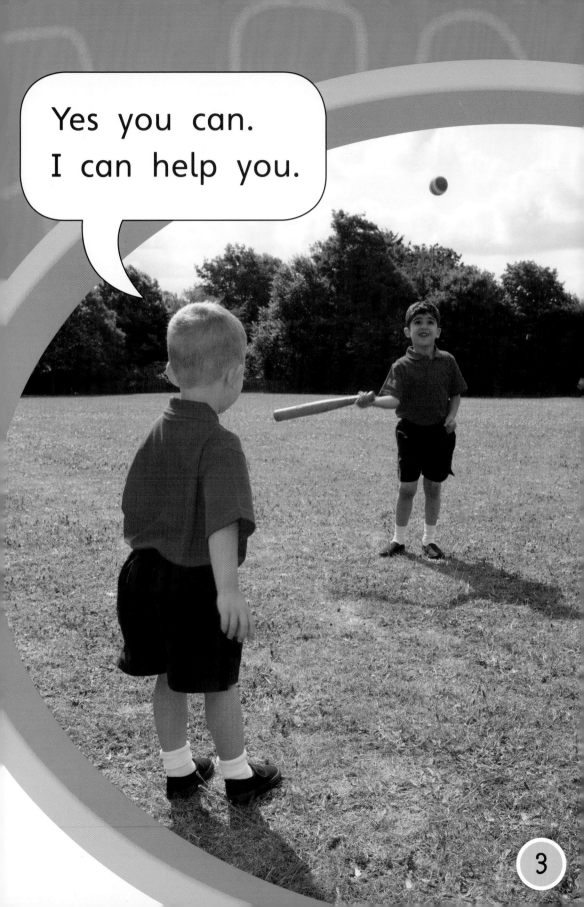

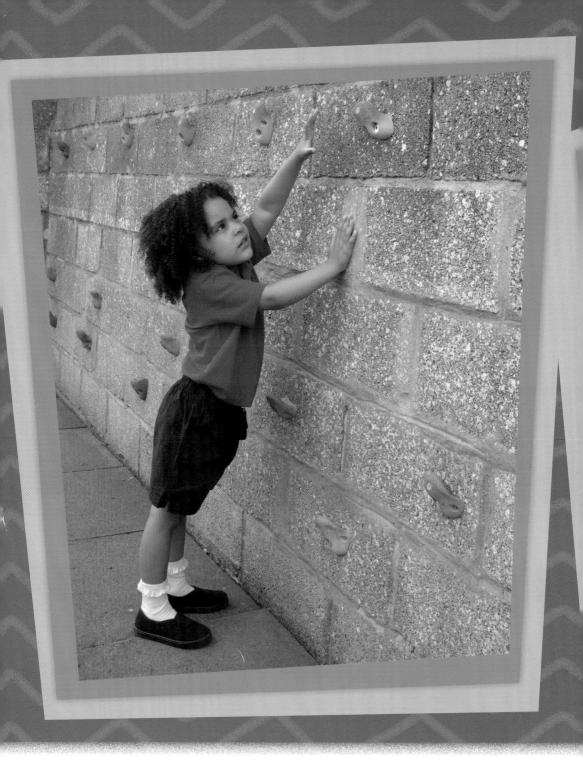

I can not get up this wall.

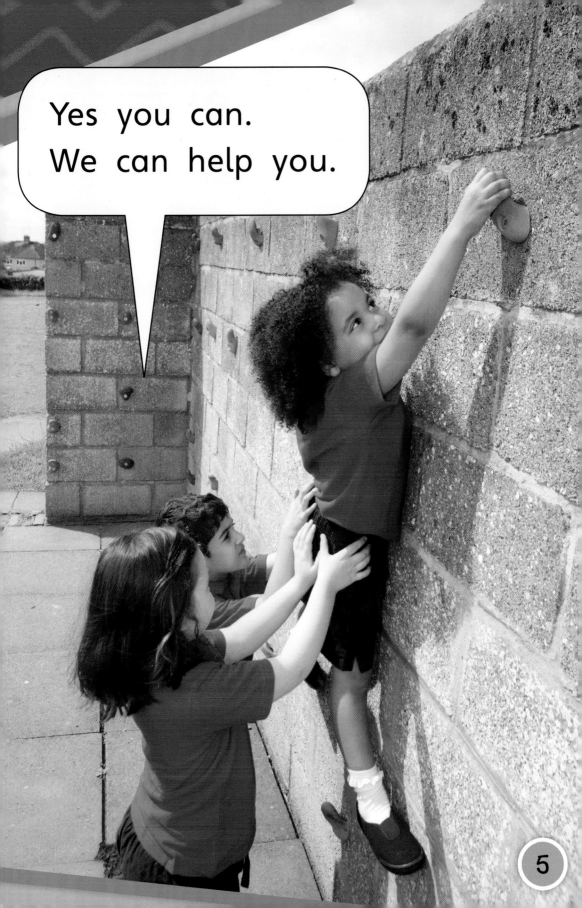

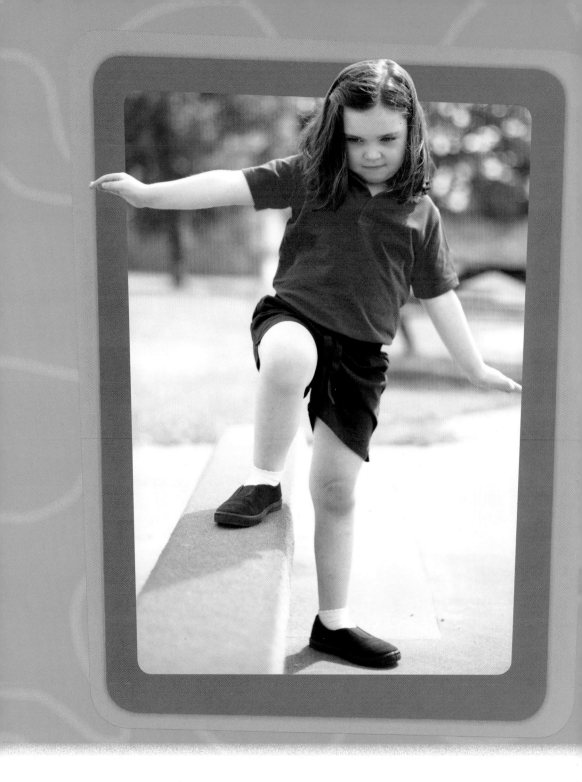

I can not walk along this bench.

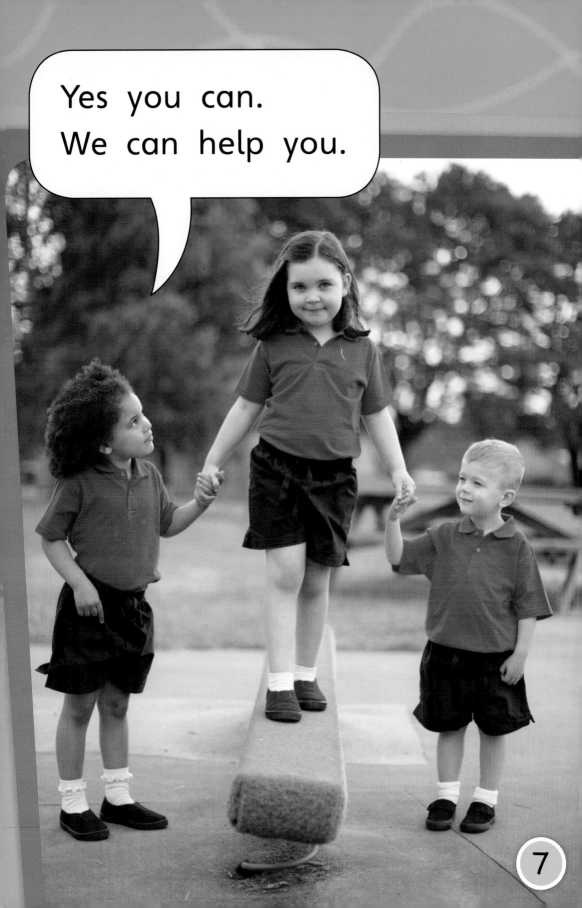

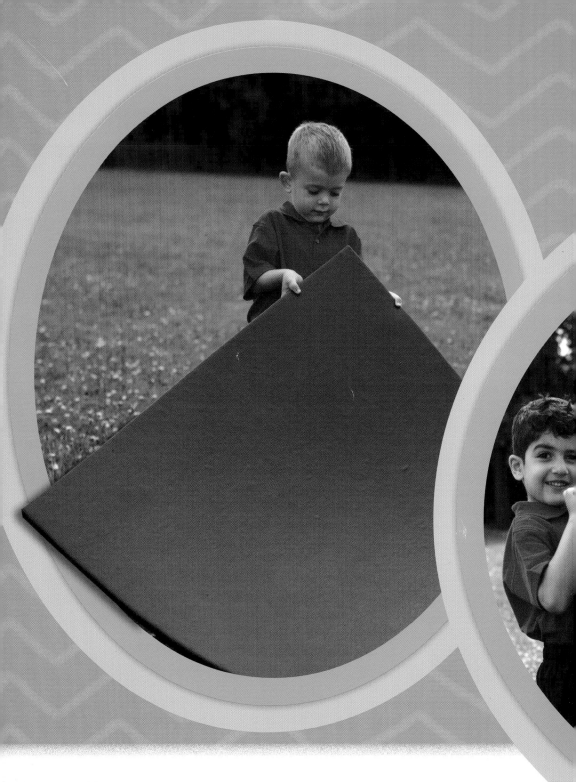

I can not pick up this mat.

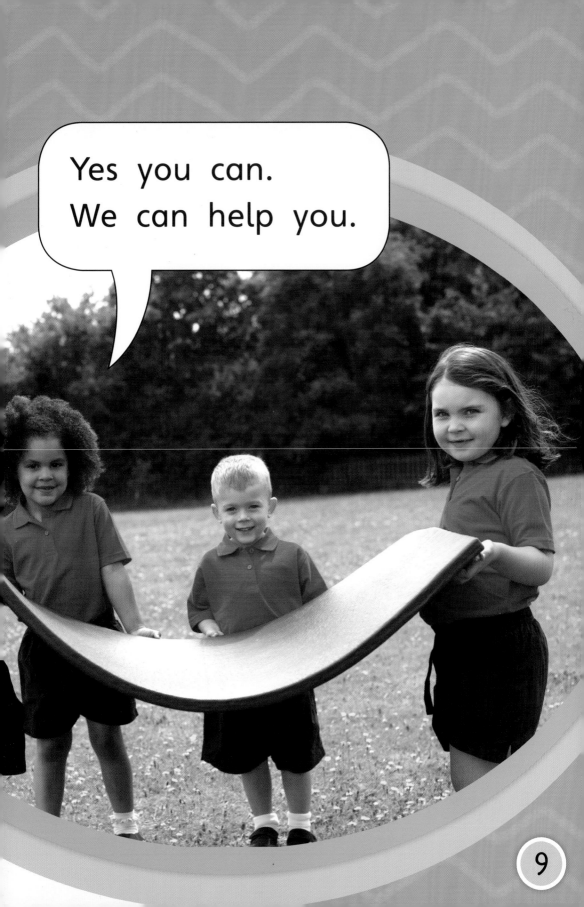

9

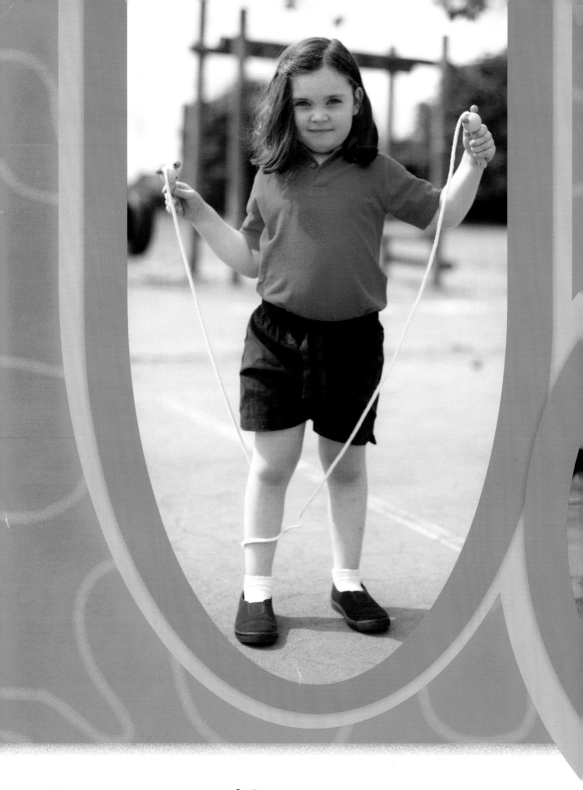

I can not skip.

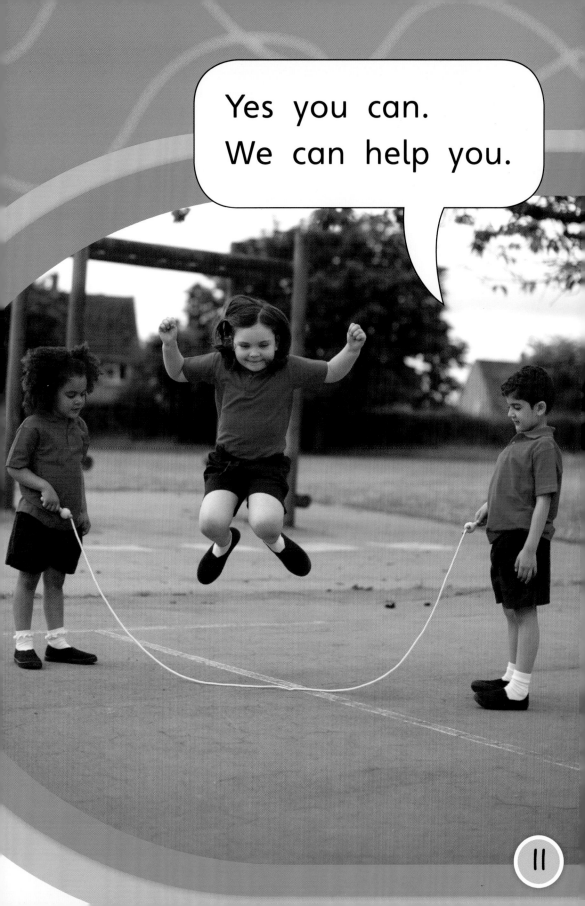

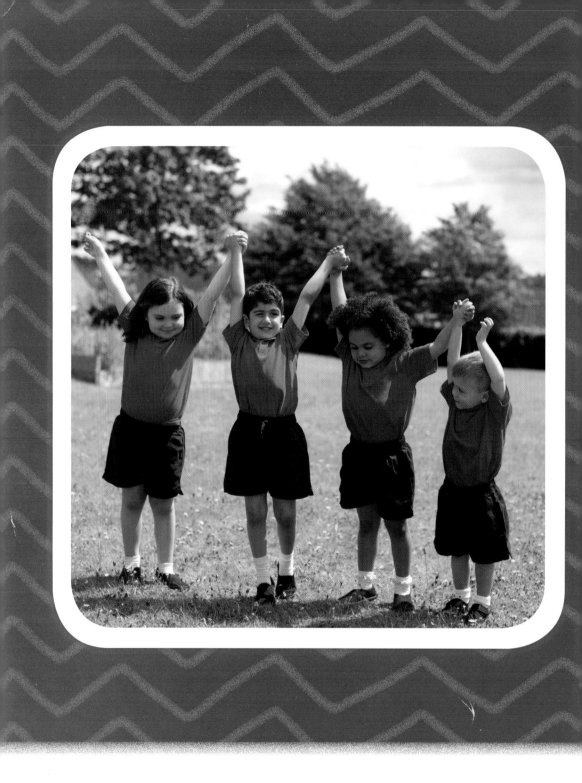

We can do it!